EASY GUITAR WITH NOTES & TAB

best of The Beach Boys

ISBN 978-0-634-03235-6

HAL•LEONARD® CORPORATION

7777 W. BLUEMOUND RD. P.O. BOX 13819 MILWAUKEE, WI 53213

Visit Hal Leonard Online at
www.halleonard.com

STRUM AND PICK PATTERNS

This chart contains the suggested strum and pick patterns that are referred to by number at the beginning of each song in this book. The symbols ⊓ and ∨ in the strum patterns refer to down and up strokes, respectively. The letters in the pick patterns indicate which right-hand fingers plays which strings.

p = **thumb**
i = **index finger**
m = **middle finger**
a = **ring finger**

For example; Pick Pattern 2
is played: thumb - index - middle - ring

Strum Patterns   Pick Patterns

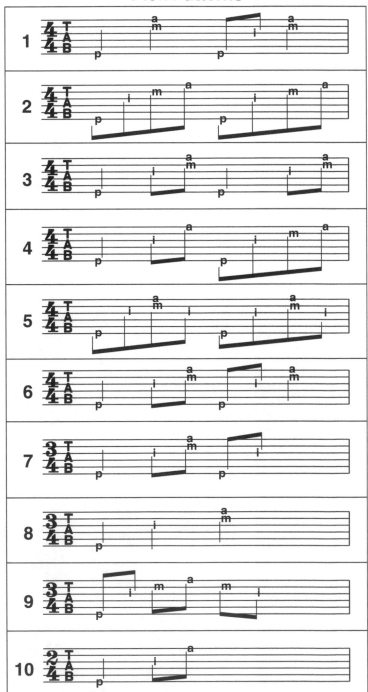

You can use the 3/4 Strum or Pick Patterns in songs written in compound meter (6/8, 9/8, 12/8, etc.).
For example, you can accompany a song in 6/8 by playing the 3/4 pattern twice in each measure.
The 4/4 Strum and Pick Patterns can be used for songs written in cut time (¢) by doubling the note
time values in the patterns. Each pattern would therefore last two measures in cut time.

California Girls

Words and Music by Brian Wilson and Mike Love

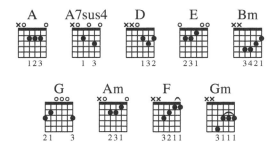

Strum Pattern: 1, 2
Pick Pattern: 2, 4

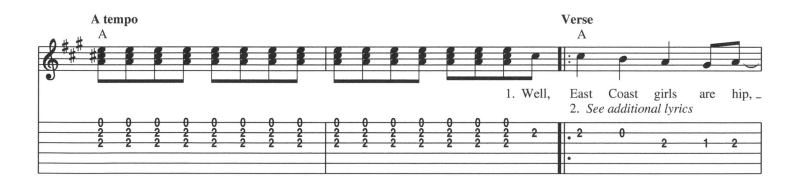

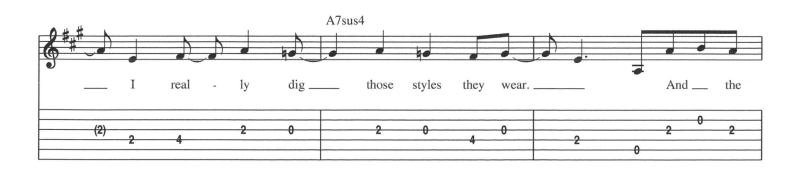

South - ern girls __ with __ the way they talk __ they knock me out when I'm __ down __ there. __

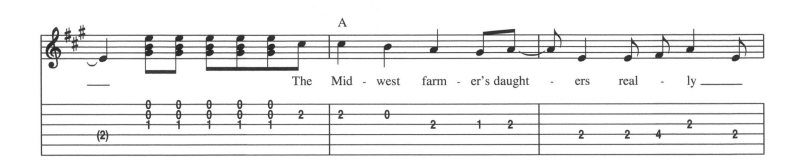

__ The Mid - west farm - er's daught - ers real - ly __

make you feel al - right. _____ And __ the North - ern girls __ with __ the

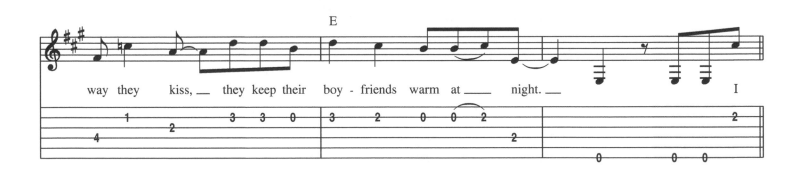

way they kiss, __ they keep their boy - friends warm at ____ night. __

Chorus

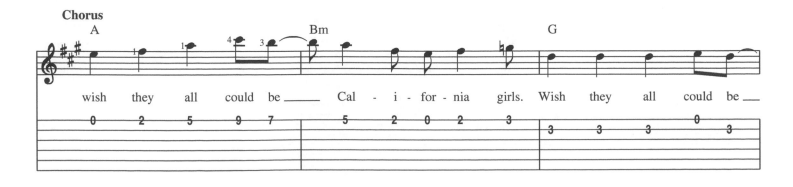

wish they all could be _____ Cal - i - for - nia girls. Wish they all could be __

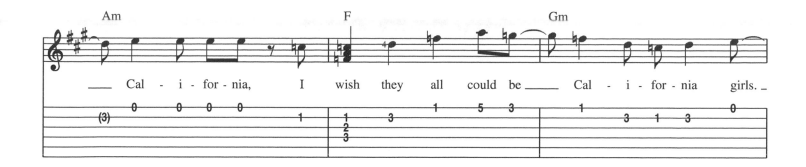

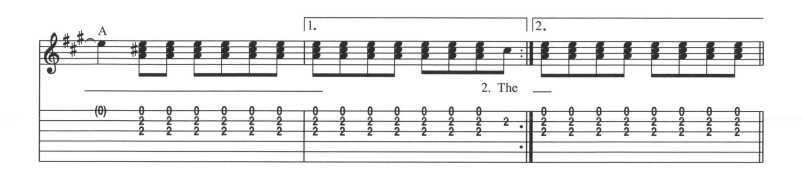

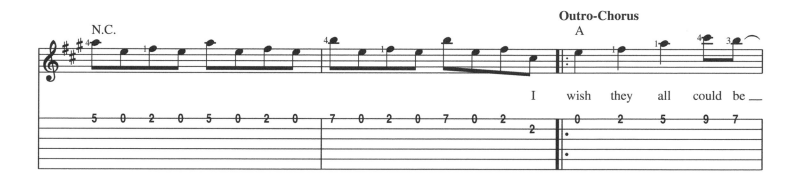

Additional Lyrics

2. The West Coast has the sunshine,
   And the girls all get so tan.
   I dig a French bikini on Hawaiian islands dolls,
   By a palm tree in the sand.
   I been all around this great big world
   And I've seen all kinds of girls.
   Yeah, but I couldn't wait to get back in the states,
   Back to the cutest girls in the world.

Barbara Ann

Words and Music by Fred Fassert

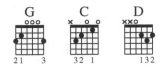

Strum Pattern: 2
Pick Pattern: 4

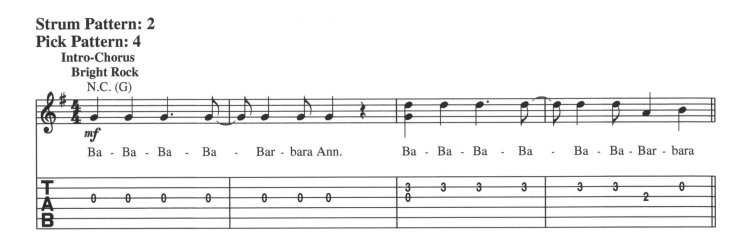

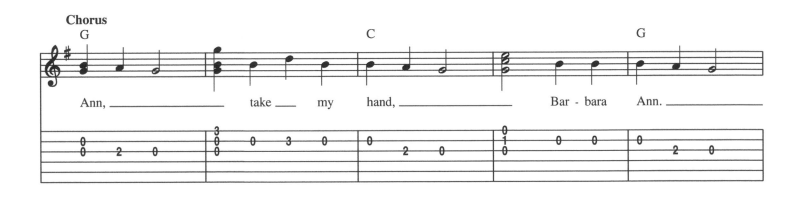

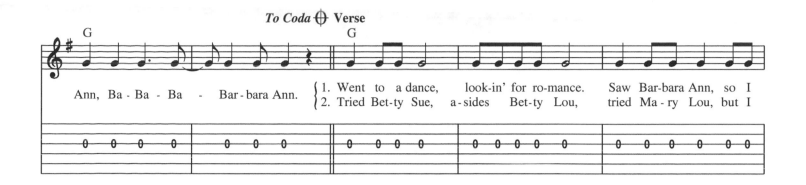

Ann, Ba - Ba - Ba - Bar-bara Ann.

1. Went to a dance, look-in' for ro-mance. Saw Bar-bara Ann, so I
2. Tried Bet-ty Sue, a-sides Bet-ty Lou, tried Ma-ry Lou, but I

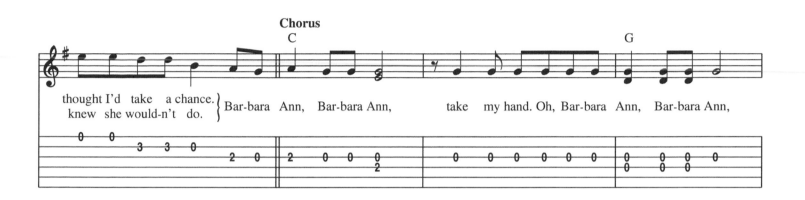

Chorus

thought I'd take a chance.) Bar-bara Ann, Bar-bara Ann, take my hand. Oh, Bar-bara Ann, Bar-bara Ann,
knew she would-n't do.

take my hand. You got me rock-in' and a-roll-in', rock-in' and a reel-in' Bar-bara

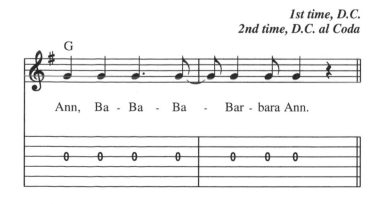

1st time, D.C.
2nd time, D.C. al Coda

Ann, Ba - Ba - Ba - Bar-bara Ann.

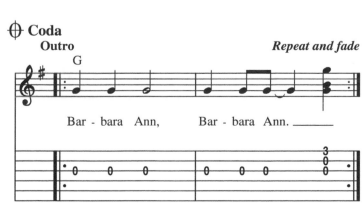

Coda

Outro

Repeat and fade

Bar-bara Ann, Bar-bara Ann. _____

Be True to Your School

Words and Music by Brian Wilson and Mike Love

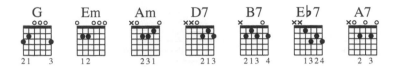

Strum Pattern: 2
Pick Pattern: 4

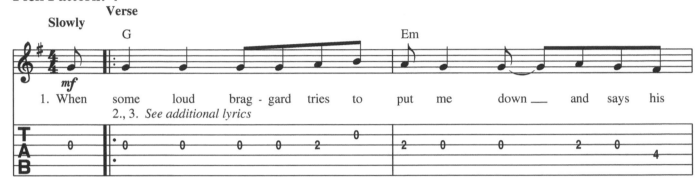

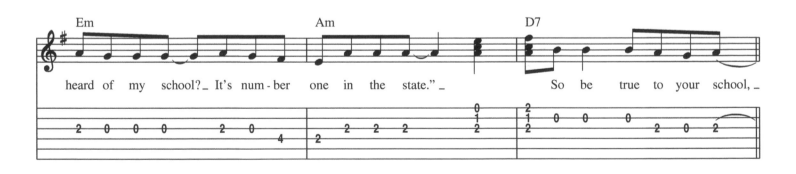

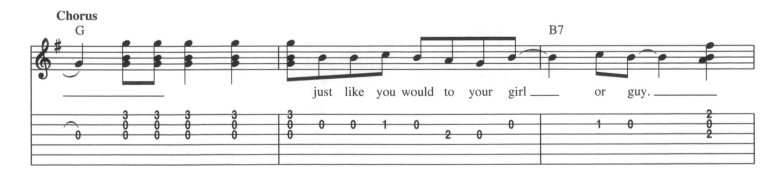

Be true to your school _____ now, _____ and let your col - ors fly. __

Be true to your school. _____

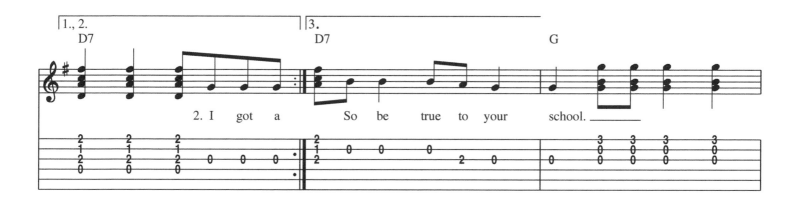

2. I got a   So be true to your   school. _____

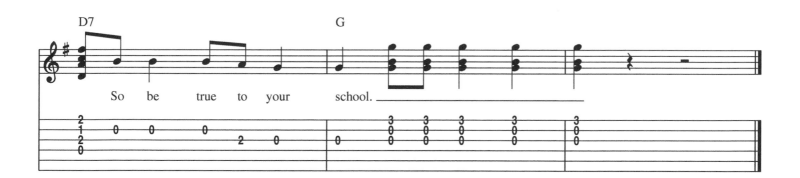

So be true to your school. _____

Additional Lyrics

2. I got a letterman's sweater with the letter in front
   I got for football and track;
   I'm proud to wear it.
   Now, when I cruise around the other parts of town
   I got my decal in back.

3. On Friday we'll be jacked up on the football game
   And I'll be ready to fight.
   We're gonna smash 'em.
   Now, my girl will be workin' on her pom-poms now,
   And she'll be yellin' tonight.

409

Words and Music by Brian Wilson, Gary Usher and Mike Love

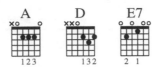

Strum Pattern: 2
Pick Pattern: 4

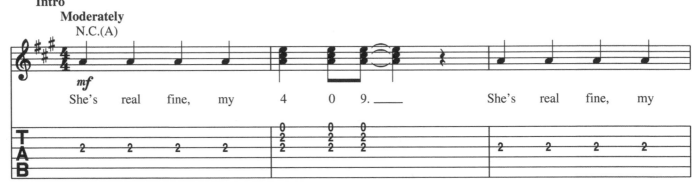

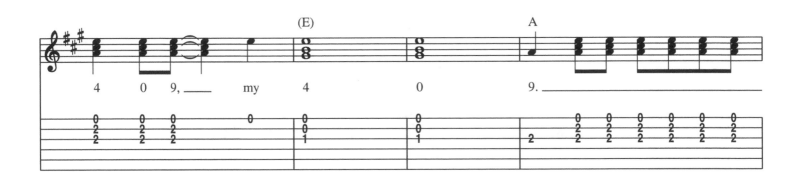

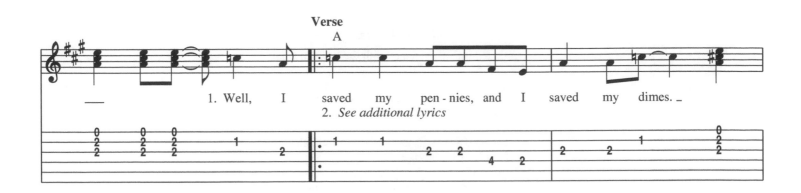

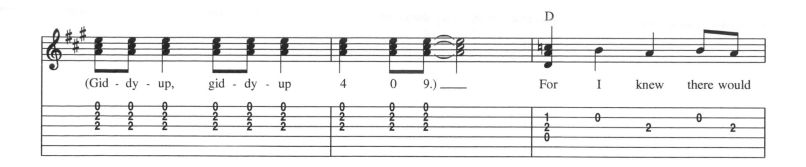

(Gid - dy - up,   gid - dy - up   4   0   9.) ___   For   I   knew   there would

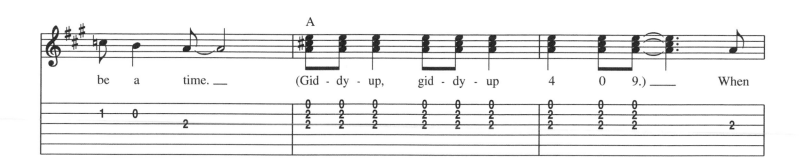

be   a   time. ___   (Gid - dy - up,   gid - dy - up   4   0   9.) ___   When

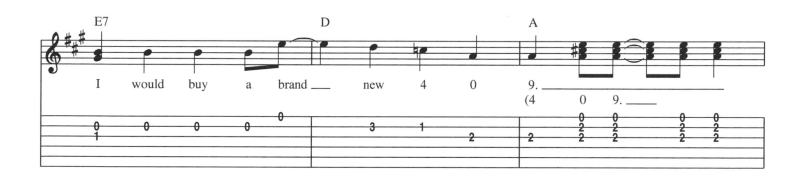

I   would   buy   a   brand ___   new   4   0   9. _____
(4   0   9. ___

Chorus

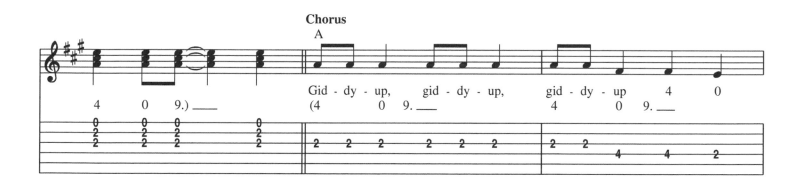

4   0   9.) ___   (4   0   9. ___   Gid - dy - up,   gid - dy - up,   gid - dy - up   4   0   4   0   9. ___

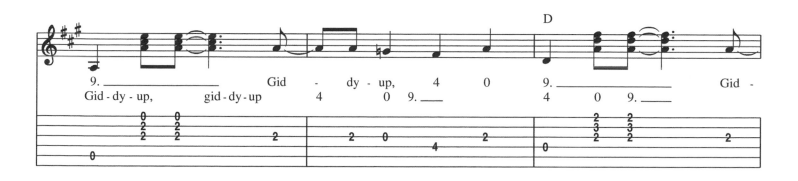

9. _____   Gid - dy - up,   4   0   9. _____   Gid -
Gid - dy - up,   gid - dy - up   4   0   9. ___   4   0   9. ___

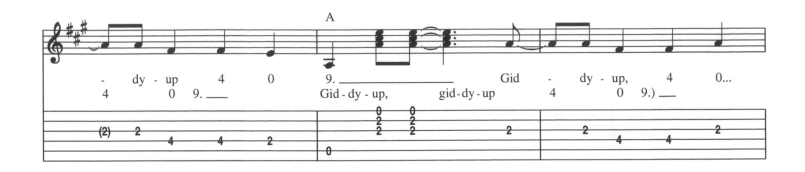

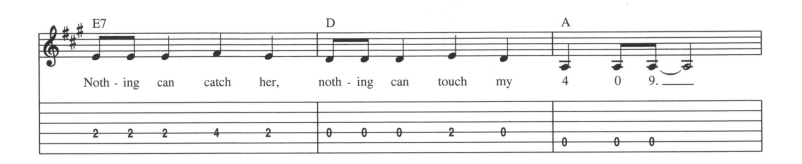

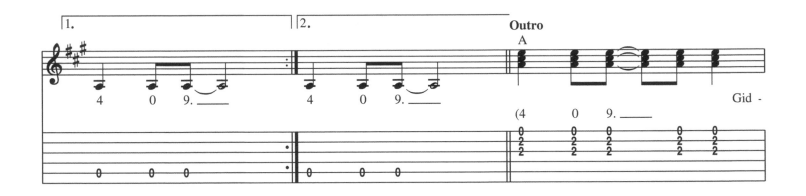

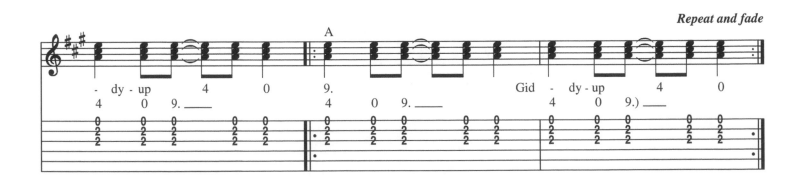

Additional Lyrics

2. When I take her to the drag, she really shines.
   (Giddy-up, giddy-up 409.)
   She always turns in the fastest time.
   (Giddy-up, giddy-up 409.)
   My four-speed, dual-quad, posi-traction 409.
   (409. 409.)

God Only Knows

Words and Music by Brian Wilson and Tony Asher

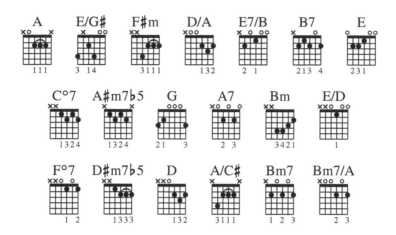

Strum Pattern: 4
Pick Pattern: 3

Intro
Moderately

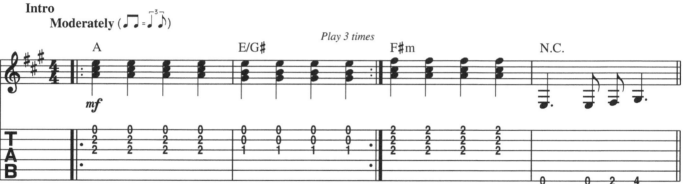

Verse

1. I may not al-ways love __ you, but long as there are __ stars a-bove you,
2. *See additional lyrics*

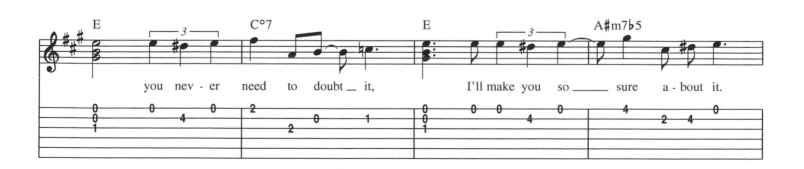

you nev-er need to doubt __ it, I'll make you so ___ sure a-bout it.

God on-ly knows _ what I'd be with-out _ you. _

Interlude

Bridge

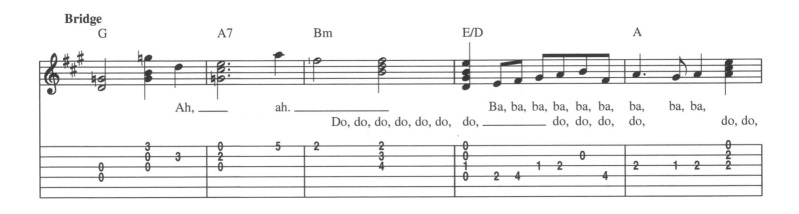

Ah, _ ah. _

Do, do, do, do, do, do, do, _ do, do, do, do, _ do, do,

Ba, ba, ba, ba, ba, ba, ba, ba, ba,

ba, ba, ba, _ ba, ba, ba, ba, ba, ba, ba, ba, ba.

do, do, do, do, do, do, do, _ do, do, do, do, ya.

Chorus

And God on-ly knows _

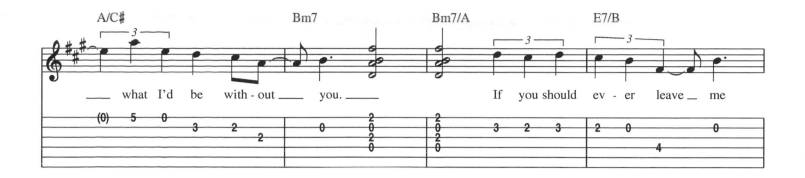

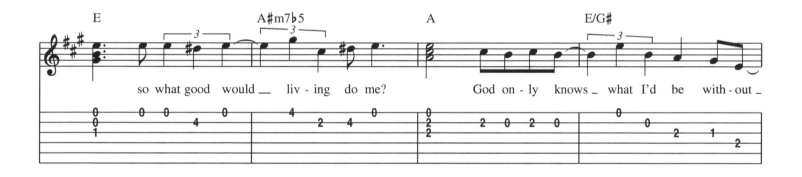

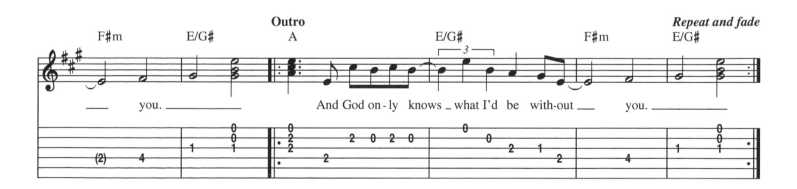

Additional Lyrics

2. If you should ever leave me,
   Well, life would still go on, believe me.
   The world could show nothing to me,
   So what good would living do me?
   God only knows what I'd be without you.

Fun, Fun, Fun

Words and Music by Brian Wilson and Mike Love

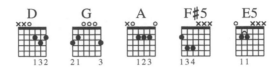

Strum Pattern: 2
Pick Pattern: 4

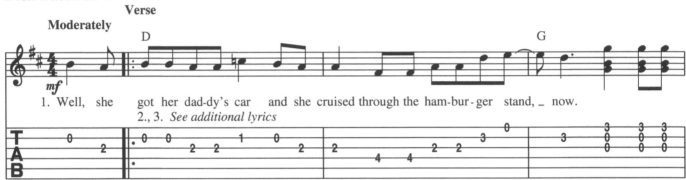

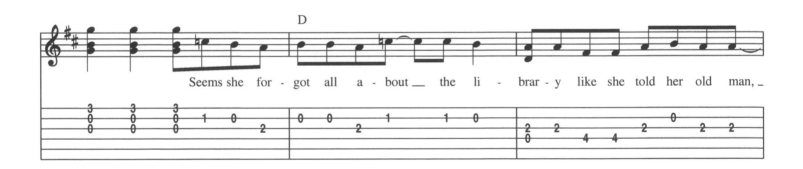

1. Well, she got her dad-dy's car and she cruised through the ham-bur-ger stand, _ now.
2., 3. *See additional lyrics*

Seems she for - got all a - bout _ the li - brar - y like she told her old man, _

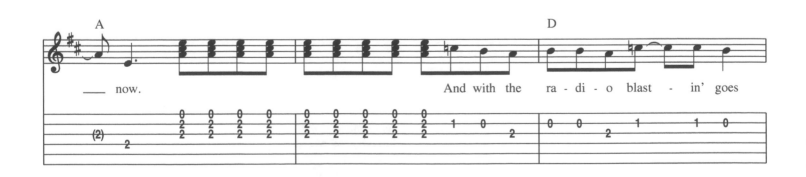

_ now.

And with the ra - di - o blast - in' goes

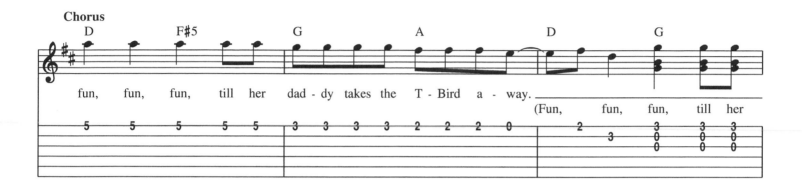

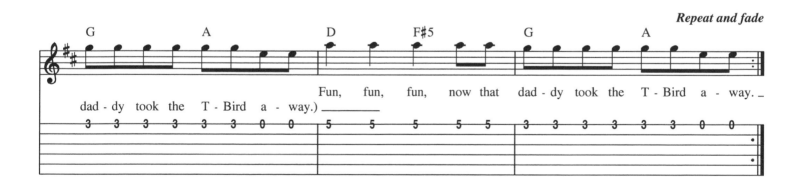

Additional Lyrics

2. Well, the girls can't stand her 'cause she walks, looks and drives like an ace, now.
   She makes the "Indy" Five Hundred look like a Roman chariot race, now.
   A lot of guys try to catch her, but she leads 'em on a wild goose chase, now.

3. Well, you knew all along that your dad was getting wise to you, now.
   And since he took your set of keys, you've been thinking that your fun is all through, now.
   But you can come along with me, 'cause we got a lot of things to do, now.

Good Vibrations

Words and Music by Brian Wilson and Mike Love

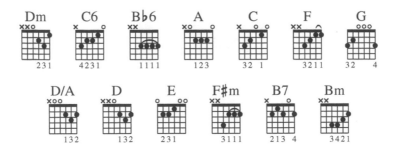

Strum Pattern: 4
Pick Pattern: 3

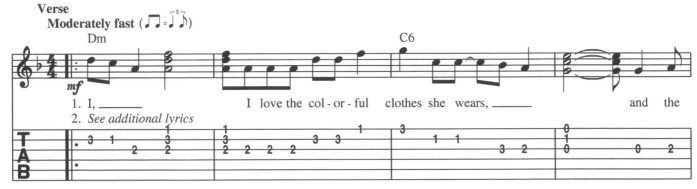

1. I, _____ I love the col - or - ful clothes she wears, _____ and the
2. *See additional lyrics*

way the sun - light plays up - on _____ her hair. _____ I _____

_____ hear the sound of a gen - tle word _____ on the wind that lifts her per - fume through the air. _____

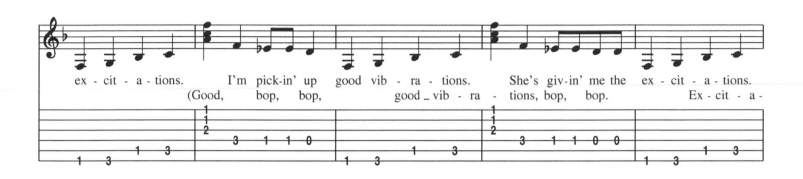

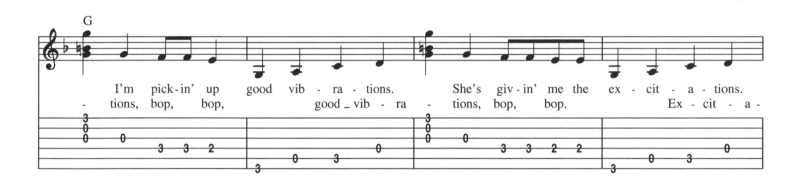

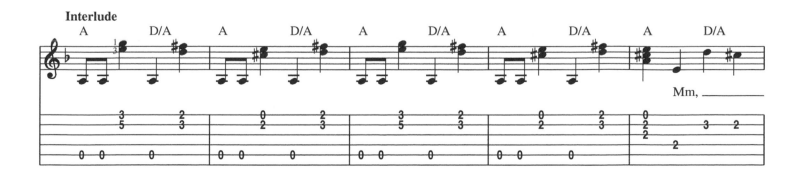

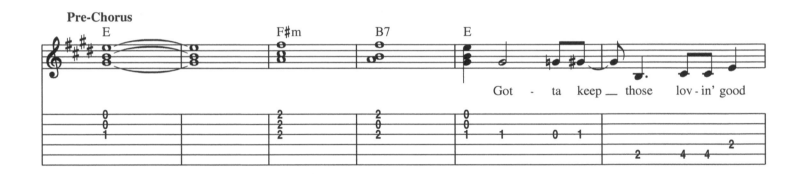

Pre-Chorus

Chorus

I'm pick-in' up good vib - ra - tions. She's giv-in' me the ex - cit - a - tions. I'm pick-in' up
(Good, bop, bop. Good _ vib - ra - tions, bop, bop. Ex - cit - a - tions, bop, bop,

good vib - ra - tions. Na, __ na. __
good _ vib - ra - tions.)

Breakdown

Na, na, na, na, na, na, na, na. __ Na, na, na, na, na, na, na, na. __

D.S. and fade

Na, na, na, na, na, na, na, na. __ Na, na, na, na, na, na, na, na. __

Additional Lyrics

2. Close my eyes, she's somehow closer now.
Softly smile I know she must be kind.
When I look in her eyes.
She goes with me to a blossom room.

Help Me Rhonda

Words and Music by Brian Wilson and Mike Love

Strum Pattern: 2
Pick Pattern: 4

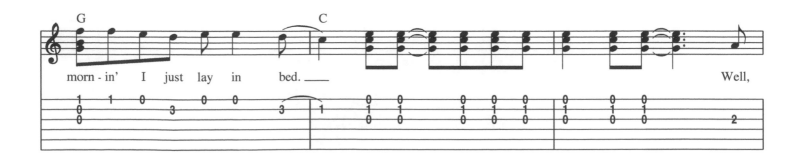

Rhon - da you look __ so fine, _____ and I know it would-n't take much time, __

_____ for you to help me Rhon - da, help __ me get her out of my heart. __

𝄋 Chorus

Help me Rhon - da, help, help me Rhon - da. Help me Rhon - da, help,

help me Rhon - da. Help me Rhon - da, help, help me Rhon - da. Help me Rhon - da, help,

help me Rhon - da. Help me Rhon - da, help, help me Rhon - da. Help me Rhon - da, help,

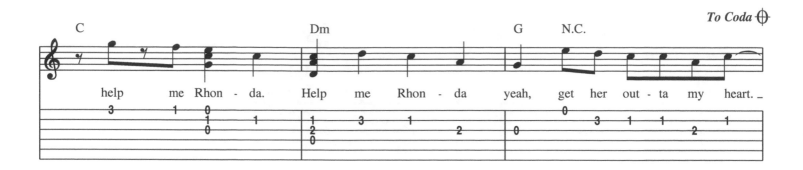

help me Rhon - da. Help me Rhon - da yeah, get her out - ta my heart. _

2. She was ___

Interlude

2nd time, D.S. al Coda

⊕ **Coda**

Outro-Chorus

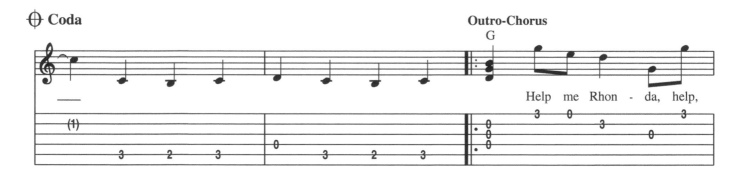

Help me Rhon - da, help,

Repeat and fade

help me Rhon - da. Help me Rhon - da, help, help me Rhon - da.

Additional Lyrics

2. She was gonna be my wife and I was gonna be her man.
   But she let another guy come between us and he shattered our plans.
   Well, Rhonda you caught my eye, and I can give you lots of reasons why
   You gotta help me Rhonda, help me get her out of my heart.

Little Deuce Coupe

Music by Brian Wilson
Words by Roger Christian

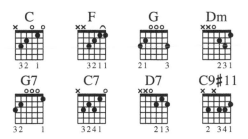

Strum Pattern: 2, 3
Pick Pattern: 3, 4

Verse
Moderate Rock

1. Well, I'm not brag-gin', babe, so don't put me down, ___ but I've got the fast-est set of
2. *See additional lyrics*

wheels in town. ___ When some-thing pulls ___ up to me, it don't e-ven try. ___ And if it

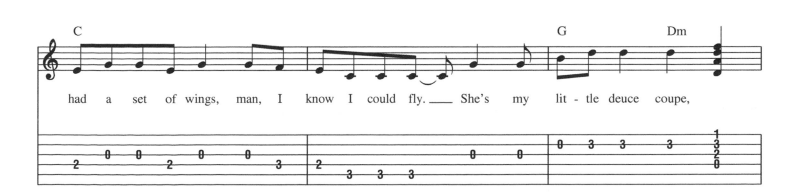

had a set of wings, man, I know I could fly. ___ She's my lit-tle deuce coupe,

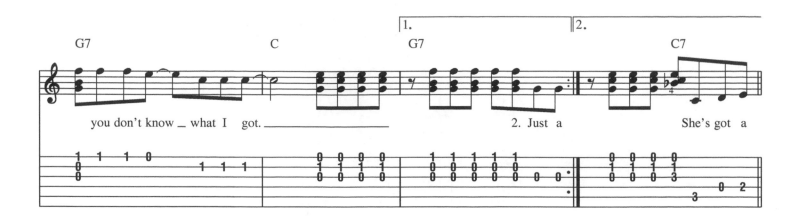

you don't know — what I got. _____ 2. Just a   She's got a

Bridge

com-pe-ti-tion clutch, with   four   on   the   floor — yeah,   she   purrs   like   a   kit-ten   till the

lake   pipes   roar. —   And   if   that   ain't   e-nough   to   make   you   flip   your   wig, —   there's

Outro

one   more   thing, I've   got   the   pink   slip,   dad-dy!   And   com-in'   off   the   line,   when   the

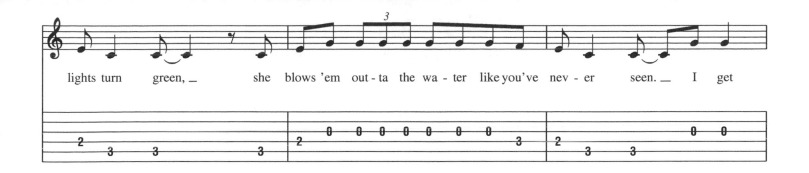

lights turn green, __ she blows 'em out-ta the wa-ter like you've nev-er seen. __ I get

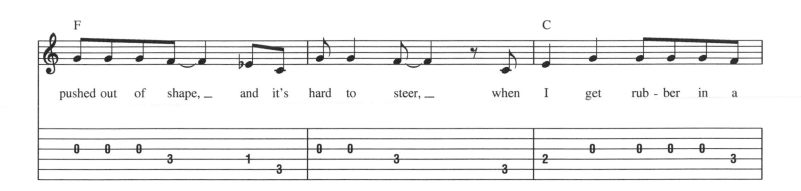

pushed out of shape, __ and it's hard to steer, __ when I get rub-ber in a

all four gears. __ She's my lit-tle deuce coupe, you don't know __ what I've got. __

She's got a

Additional Lyrics

2. Just a little deuce coupe with a flathead mill,
   But she'll walk a Thunderbird like it's standin' still.
   She's ported and relieved, and she's stroked and she's bored.
   She'll do a hundred and forty with the top end floored.
   She's my little deuce coupe,
   You don't know what I got.

I Get Around

Words and Music by Brian Wilson and Mike Love

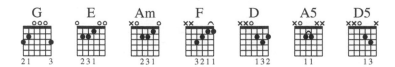

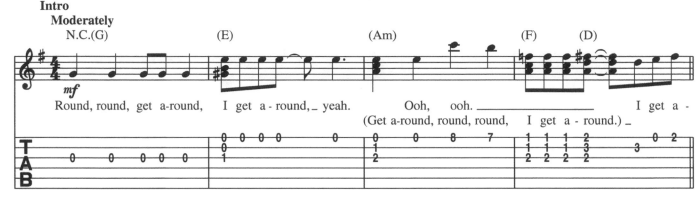

Strum Pattern: 2
Pick Pattern: 4

Intro
Moderately

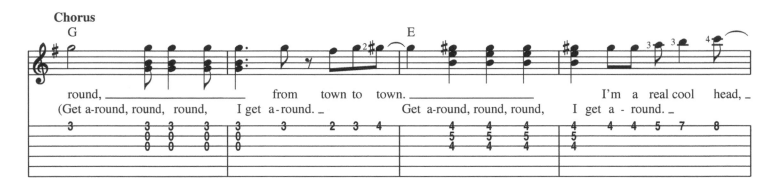

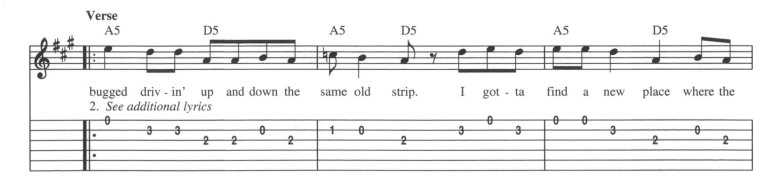

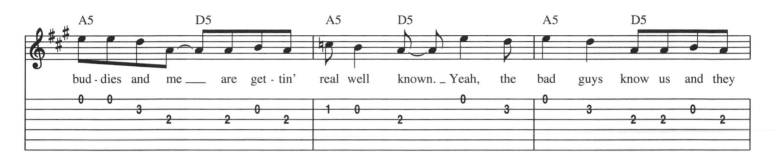

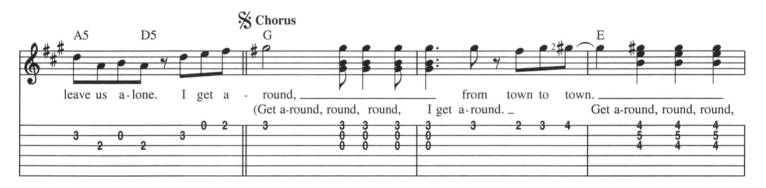

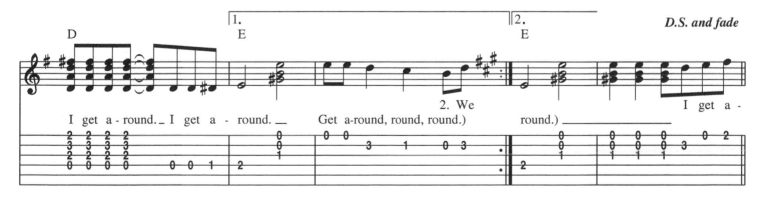

Additional Lyrics

2. We always take my car 'cause it's never been beat.
   And we've never missed yet with the girls we meet.
   None of the guys go steady 'cause it wouldn't be right
   To leave their best girl home on a Saturday night.

In My Room

Words and Music by Brian Wilson and Gary Usher

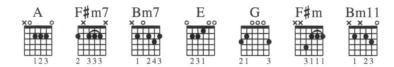

Strum Pattern: 8
Pick Pattern: 8

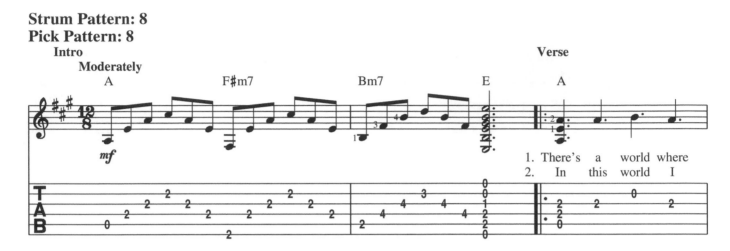

1. There's a world where
2. In this world I

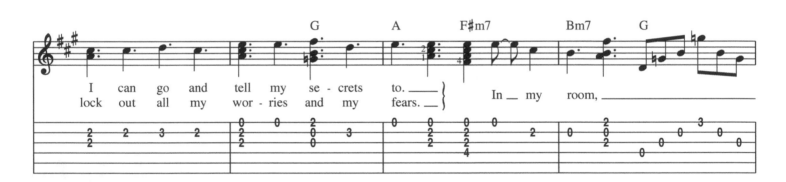

I can go and tell my se-crets to. _____
lock out all my wor-ries and my fears. _____
In _ my room, _____

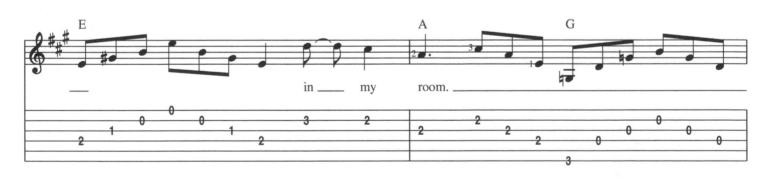

_ in _ my room. _____

Bridge

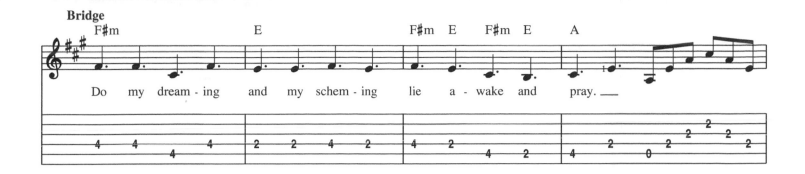

Do my dream-ing and my schem-ing lie a-wake and pray. ___

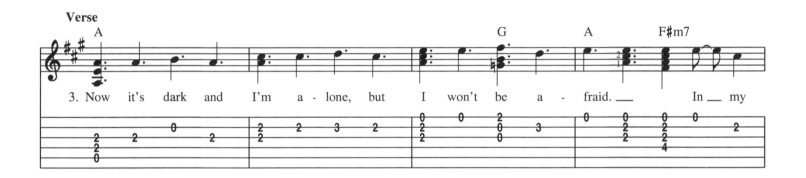

Do my cry-ing and my sigh-ing, laugh at yes-ter-day. ___

Verse

3. Now it's dark and I'm a-lone, but I won't be a-fraid. ___ In ___ my

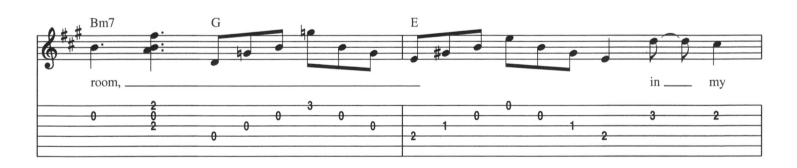

room, ___ in ___ my

Outro

Repeat and fade

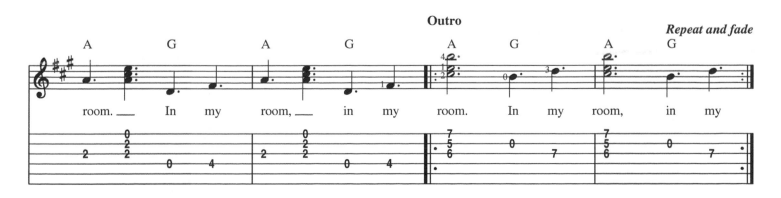

room. ___ In my room, ___ in my room. In my room, in my

Kokomo

from the Motion Picture COCKTAIL

Words and Music by Mike Love, Terry Melcher, John Phillips and Scott McKenzie

Strum Pattern: 3
Pick Pattern: 3

Intro

Moderately bright

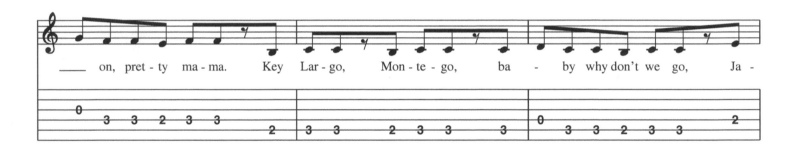

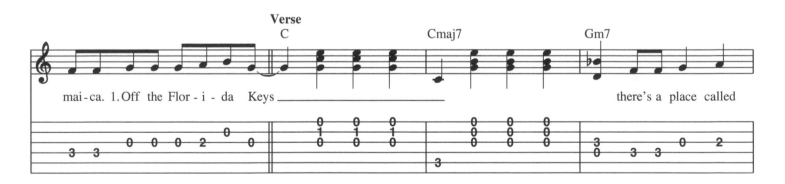

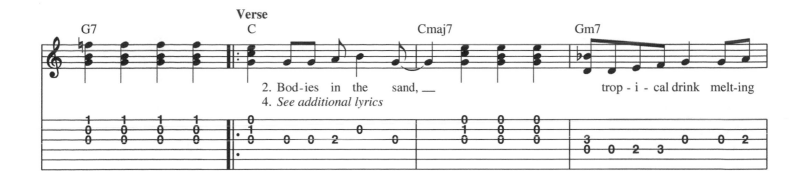

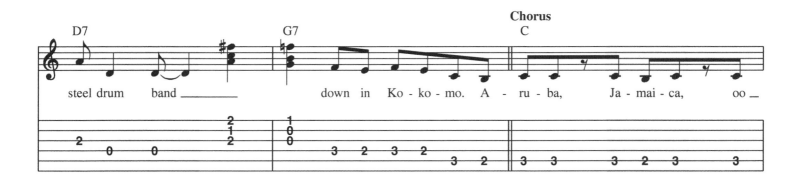

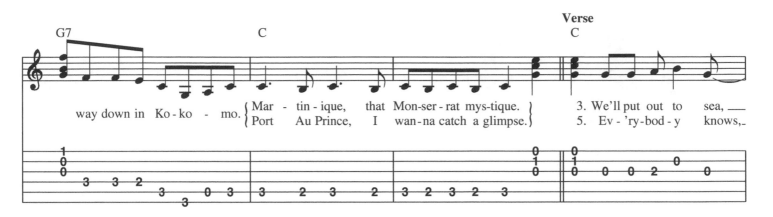

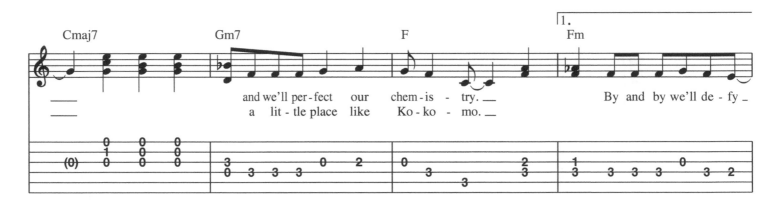

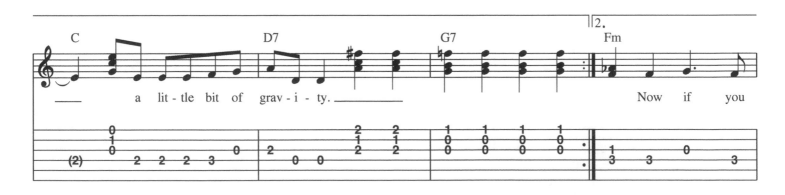

Outro-Chorus

ru - ba, Ja - mai - ca, oo ___ I wan - na take ya to Ber - mu - da, Ba - ha - ma, come __

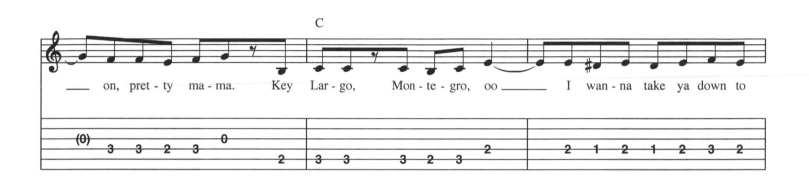

___ on, pret - ty ma - ma. Key Lar - go, Mon - te - gro, oo ___ I wan - na take ya down to

Ko - ko - mo, ___ we'll get there fast ___ and then we'll take it slow. ___

Repeat and fade

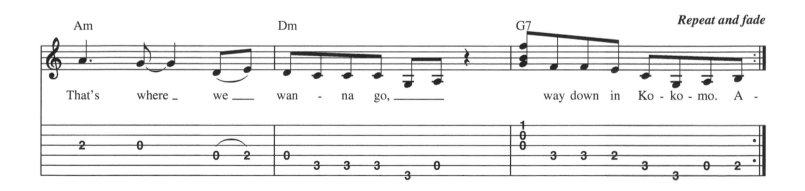

That's where __ we __ wan - na go, ___ way down in Ko - ko - mo. A -

Additional Lyrics

4. Afternoon delight,
   Cocktails and moonlit nights.
   That dreamy look in your eye
   Gives me a tropical contact high,
   Way down in Kokomo.

Shut Down

Words by Roger Christian
Music by Brian Wilson

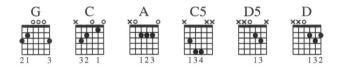

Strum Pattern: 2, 6
Pick Pattern: 3, 4

Intro
Bright Rock

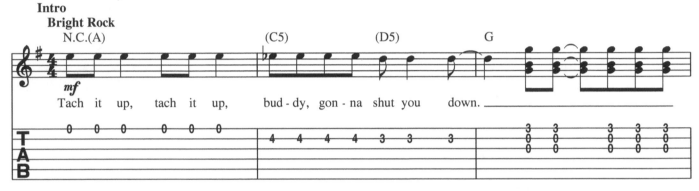

Tach it up, tach it up, bud-dy, gon-na shut you down. _____

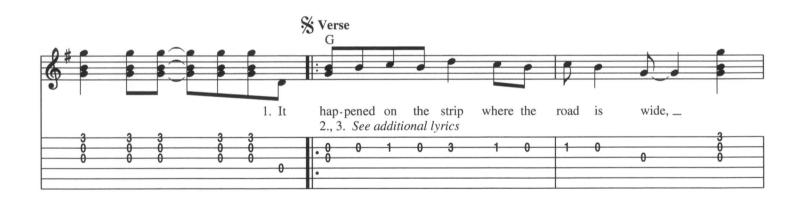

1. It hap-pened on the strip where the road is wide, _
2., 3. *See additional lyrics*

two cool shorts stand-in' side by side. _ Yeah, my fuel-in-ject-ed Sting-ray and a

Four - thir - teen, ____ rev - in' up our en - gines and it sounds real mean. _____

To Coda ⊕

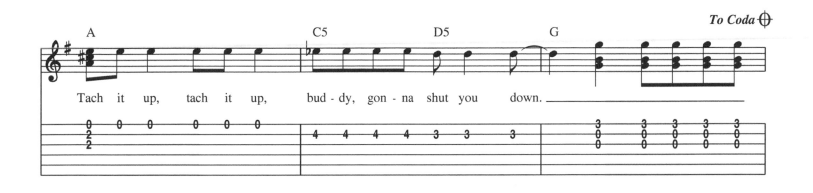

Tach it up, tach it up, bud - dy, gon - na shut you down. _____

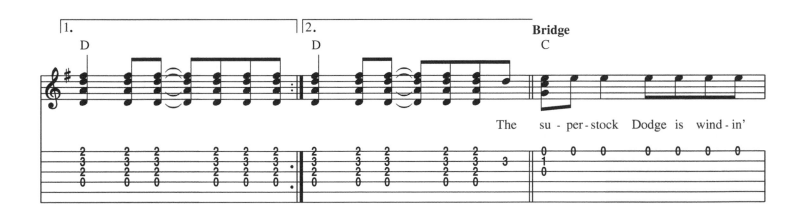

The su - per - stock Dodge is wind - in'

out in low, __ but my fuel - in - ject - ed Sting-ray's real - ly start - in' to go. __ To

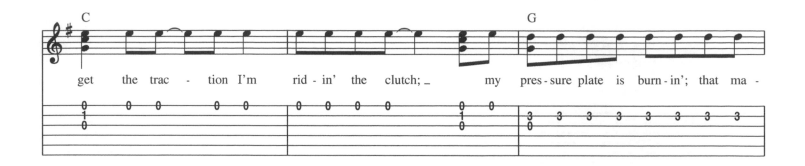

get the trac - tion I'm rid - in' the clutch; _ my pres - sure plate is burn - in'; that ma -

D.S. al Coda

⊕ **Coda**

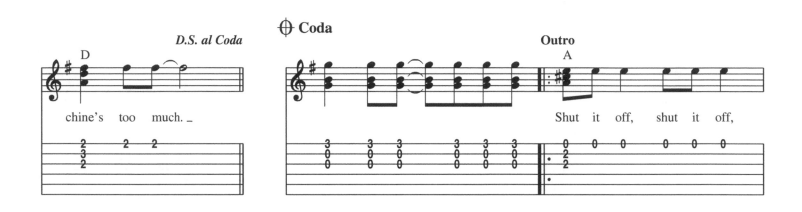

chine's too much. _

Outro

Shut it off, shut it off,

Repeat and fade

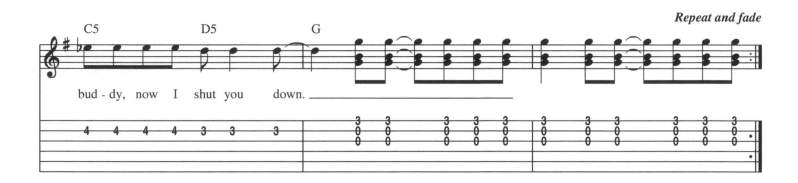

bud - dy, now I shut you down. _____

Additional Lyrics

2. Declinin' numbers at an even rate,
   At the count of one we both accelerate.
   My Stingray is light, the slicks are startin' to spin,
   But the Four-thirteen's really diggin' in.
   Gotta be cool now, power shift, here we go.

3. Pedal's to the floor, hear his dual quads drive,
   And now the Four-thirteen's lead is startin' to shrink.
   He's hot with ram induction, but it's understood.
   I got a fuel-injected engine sittin' under my hood.
   Shut it off, shut if off, buddy, now I shut you down.

Sloop John B

Words and Music by Brian Wilson

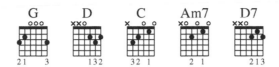

Strum Pattern: 6
Pick Pattern: 4

Verse
Moderately

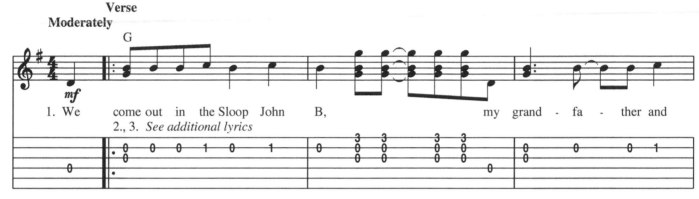

1. We come out in the Sloop John B,
   my grand - fa - ther and
2., 3. *See additional lyrics*

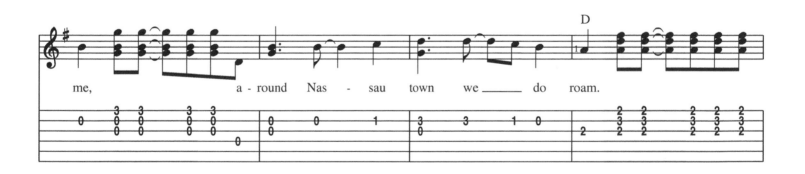

me, a - round Nas - sau town we _____ do roam.

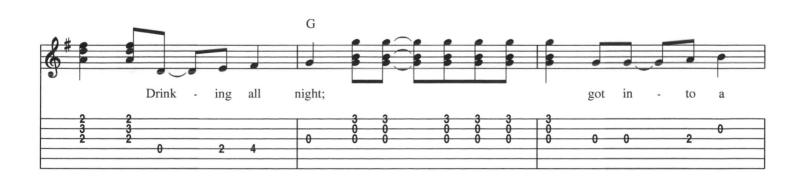

Drink - ing all night; got in - to a

fight.   Well, I feel so broke _ up,   I wan - na go

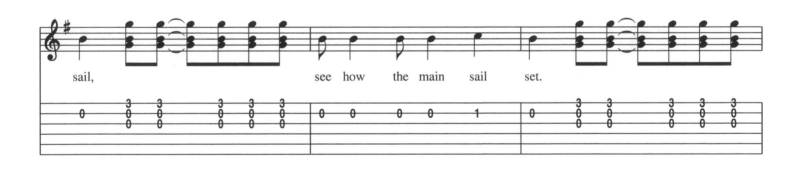

home.   So hoist up the John   B

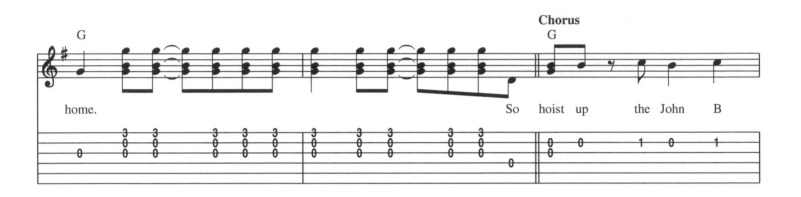

sail,   see how the main sail set.

Call for the Cap - tain a - shore, let ___ me go home. _____

Let ___ me go home,   I wan - na go

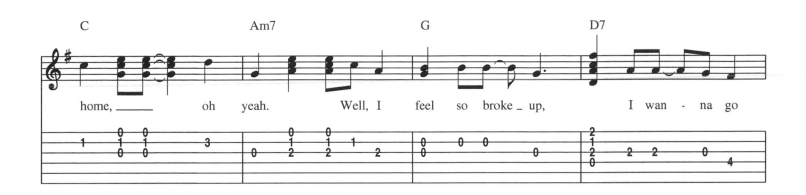

home, _____ oh yeah.   Well, I feel so broke _ up,   I wan - na go

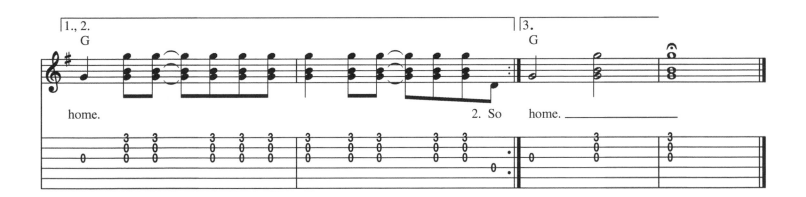

home.   2. So home. _____

Additional Lyrics

2. So first mate, he got drunk,
   He broke in the Captain's trunk.
   The constable had to come and take him away.
   Sheriff John Stone,
   Why don't you leave me alone?
   Well, I feel so broke up, I wanna go home.

3. The poor cook, he got the fits,
   He threw away all my grits
   And then he took and he ate up all of my corn.
   Let me go home.
   Why don't they let me go home?
   This is the worst trip I've ever been on.

Surfer Girl

Words and Music by Brian Wilson

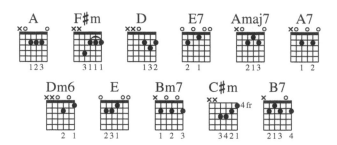

Strum Pattern: 8
Pick Pattern: 8

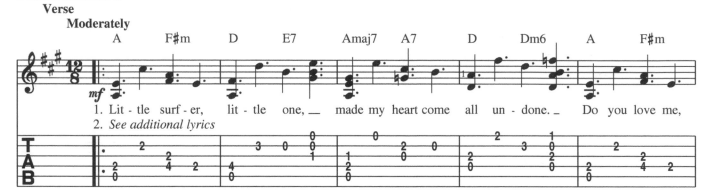

1. Lit - tle surf - er, lit - tle one, __ made my heart come all un - done. __ Do you love me,
2. *See additional lyrics*

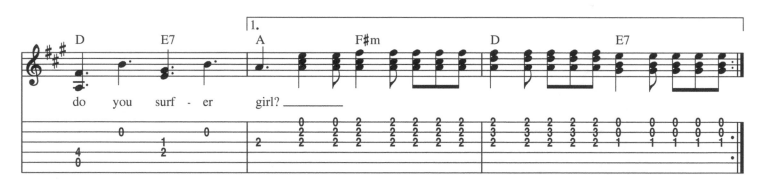

do you surf - er girl? _____

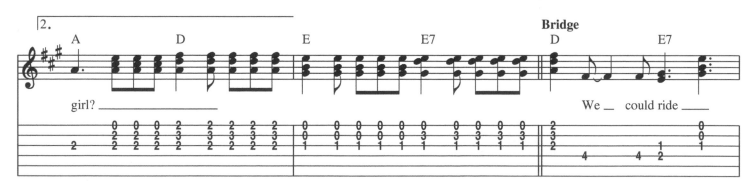

girl? _____ We __ could ride __

the surf to - geth - er __ while our love __ would grow. _____

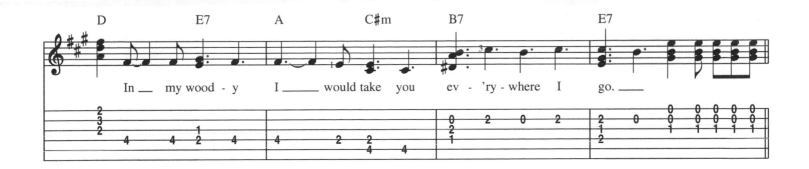

In — my wood - y I — would take you ev - 'ry - where I go. —

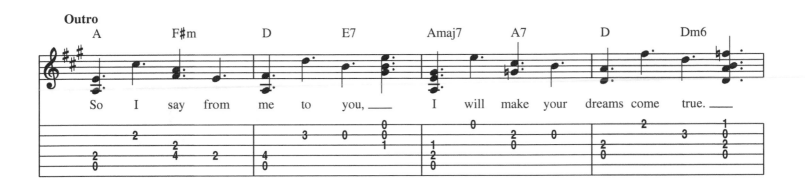

Outro

So I say from me to you, — I will make your dreams come true. —

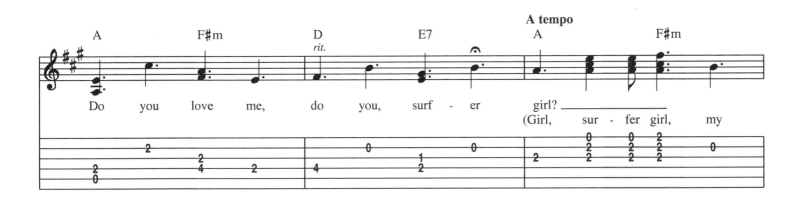

rit.   **A tempo**

Do you love me, do you, surf - er girl? —
(Girl, sur - fer girl, my

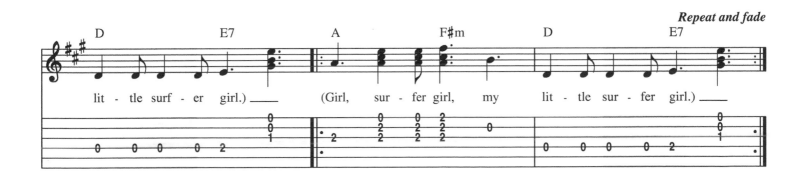

Repeat and fade

lit - tle surf - er girl.) — (Girl, sur - fer girl, my lit - tle sur - fer girl.) —

Additional Lyrics

2. I have watched you on the shore,
Standing by the ocean's roar.
Do you love me, do you surfer girl?

Surfin'

Words and Music by Brian Wilson and Mike Love

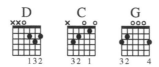

Strum Pattern: 2
Pick Pattern: 4

Intro
Moderately

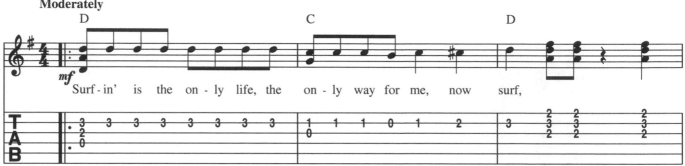

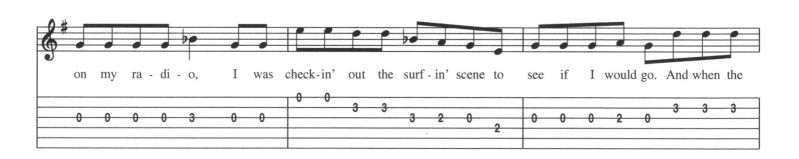

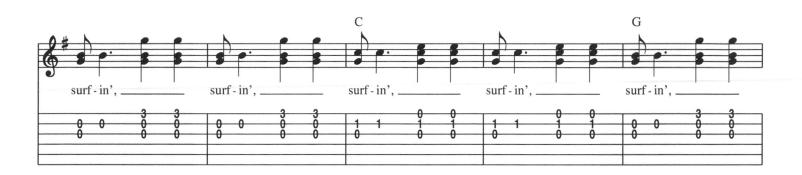

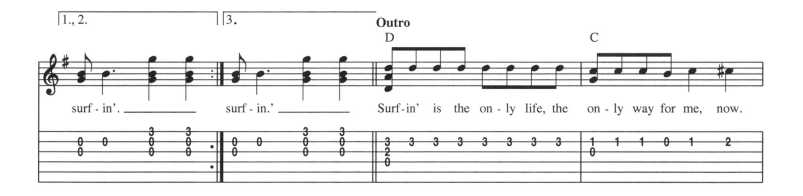

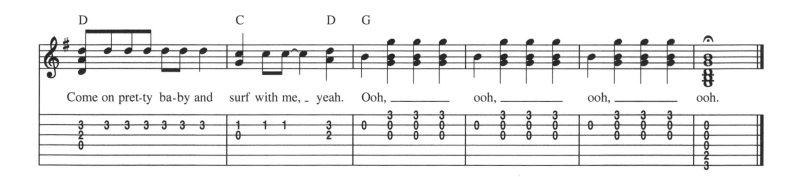

Additional Lyrics

2. From the early mornin' to the middle of the night,
   Any time the surf is up, the time is right.
   And when the surf is down, to take its place,
   We'll do the surfer stomp; it's the latest dance craze.

3. Now the dawn is breakin' and we really gotta go.
   But we'll be back here very soon; that you better know.
   Yeah, my surfer knots are risin' and my board is losin' wax,
   But that won't stop me, baby, 'cause you know I'm comin' back.

Surfin' Safari

Words and Music by Brian Wilson and Mike Love

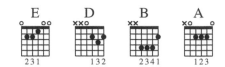

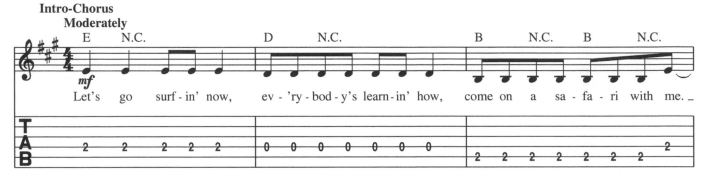

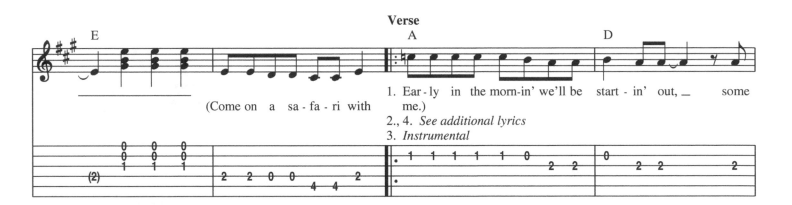

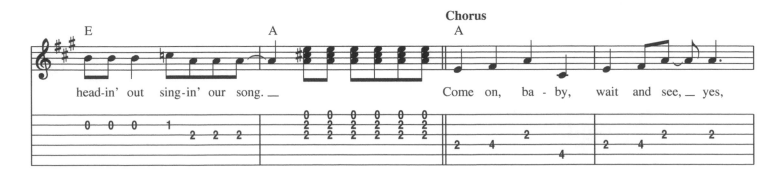

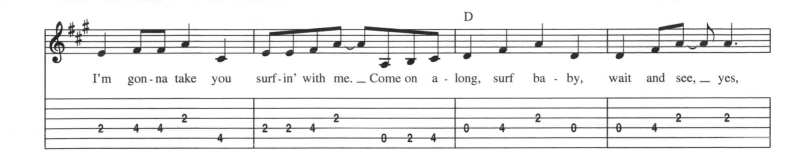

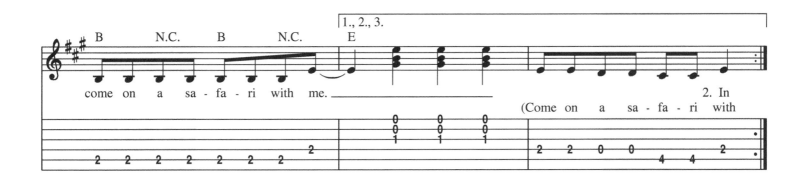

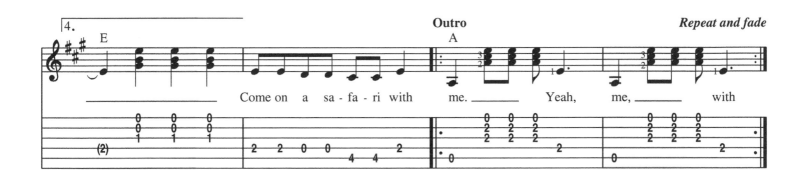

Additional Lyrics

2. In Huntington and Malibu they're shootin' the pier,
   In Rincon, they're walkin' the nose.
   We're goin' on safari to the islands this year,
   So if you're comin', get ready to go.

4. They're anglin' in Laguna and Cerro Azul,
   They're kickin' out in Dohini too.
   I'll tell you surfin's runnin' wild, it's gettin' bigger ev'ry day
   From Hawaii to the shores of Peru.

Wouldn't It Be Nice

Words and Music by Brian Wilson, Tony Asher and Mike Love

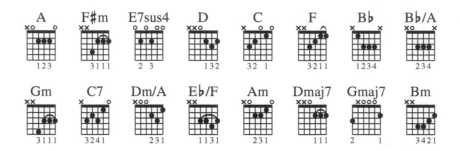

Strum Pattern: 2
Pick Pattern: 4

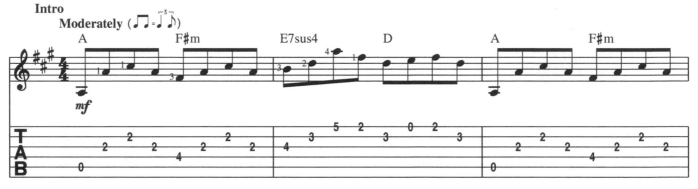

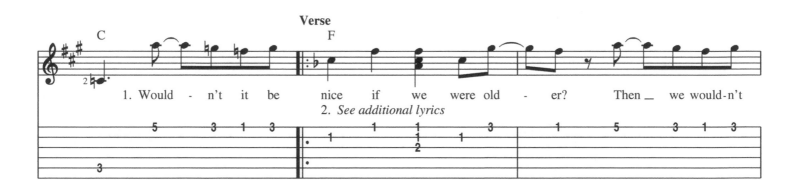

-er in ___ the kind of world where we'd __ be - long? _____

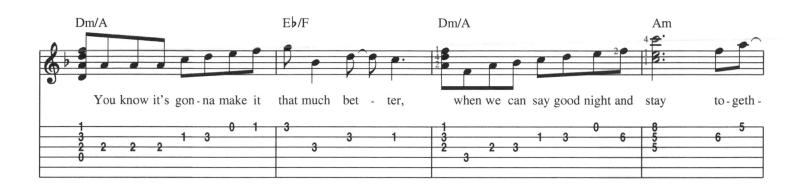

You know it's gon - na make it that much bet - ter, when we can say good night and stay to - geth-

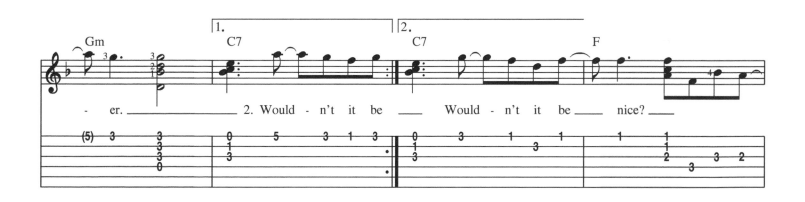

-er. _____ 2. Would - n't it be ____ Would - n't it be ____ nice? ____

Bridge

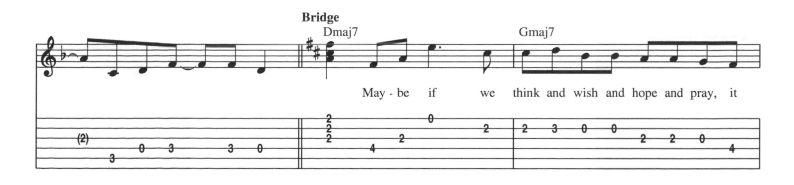

May - be if we think and wish and hope and pray, it

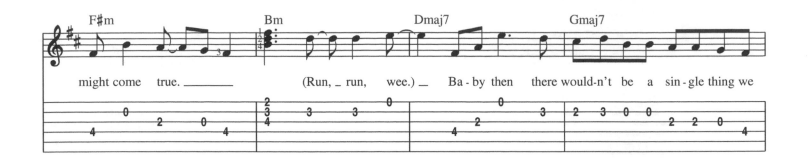

might come true. _____ (Run, _ run, wee.) _ Ba - by then there would-n't be a sin - gle thing we

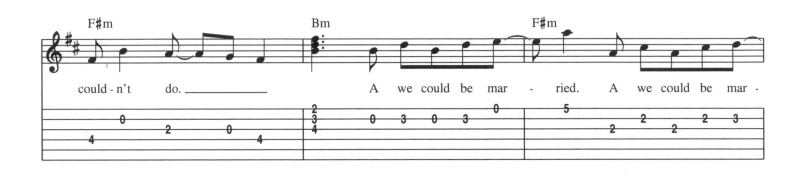

could - n't do. _____ A we could be mar - ried. A we could be mar -

- ried and then we'd be hap - py, and then we'd be hap - py. A would-n't it be __

__ nice? _____ (Ba, ba, ba. _ Be, doo, be, doo. Ba, ___ ba, ba, ba, _

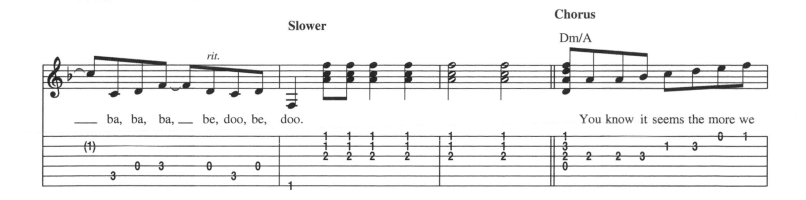

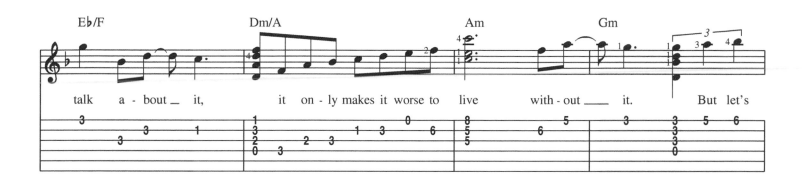

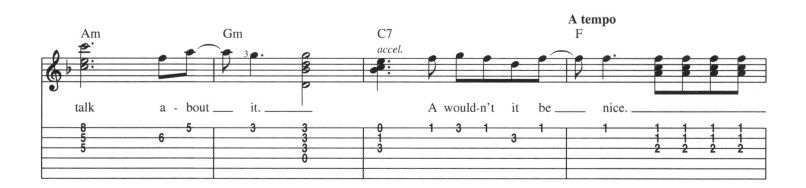

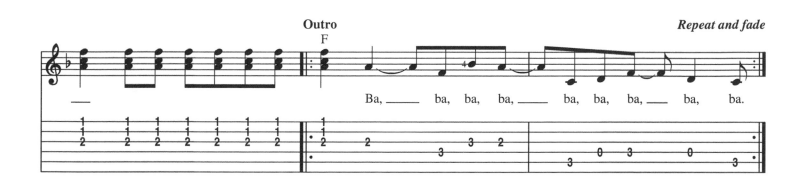

Additional Lyrics

2. Wouldn't it be nice if we could wake up
   In the morning when the day is new.
   And after havin' spent the day together,
   Hold each other close the whole night through.
   Well, happy times together, we'd be spending.
   I wish that ev'ry kiss was never ending.
   Wouldn't it be nice?

Surfin' U.S.A.

Words and Music by Chuck Berry

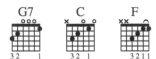

Strum Pattern: 1
Pick Pattern: 2

Intro

Moderate Rock

Verse

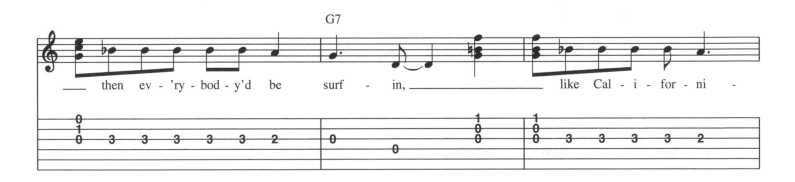

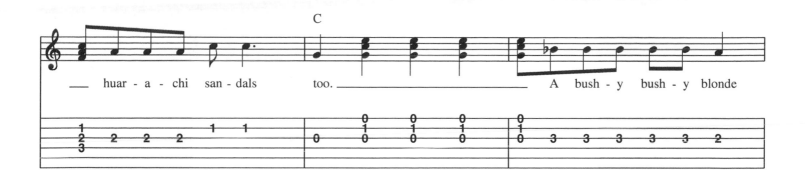

_____ huar - a - chi san - dals too. _____ A bush - y bush - y blonde

hair - do, _____ surf - in' U. S. A. _____

Verse

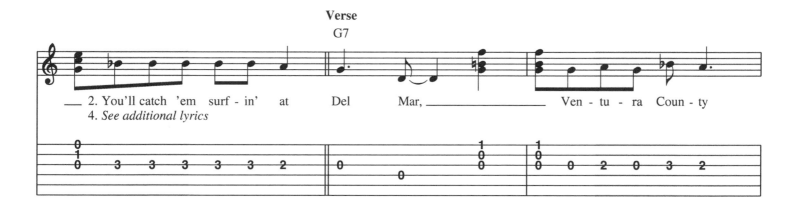

_____ 2. You'll catch 'em surf - in' at Del Mar, _____ Ven - tu - ra Coun - ty
4. *See additional lyrics*

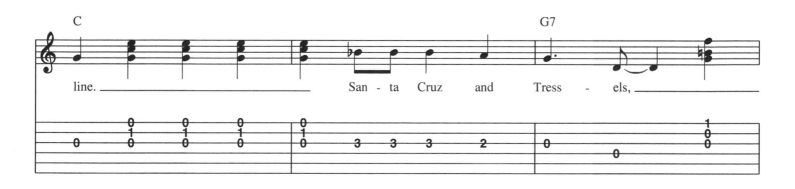

line. _____ San - ta Cruz and Tress - els, _____

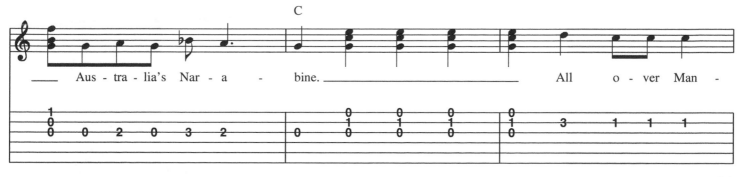

_____ Aus - tra - lia's Nar - a - bine. _____ All o - ver Man -

hat - tan _____ and down Do - he - ny way. _____

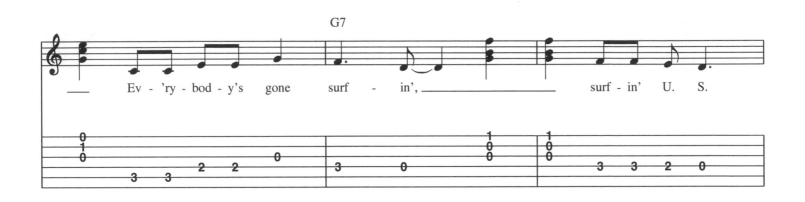

____ Ev - 'ry - bod - y's gone surf - in', _____ surf - in' U. S.

1.   2.

A. _____ 3. We'll all be plan-nin' out a   A. _____

Additional Lyrics

3. We'll all be plannin' out a route
    Were gonna take real soon.
    We're waxin' down our surfboards,
    We can't wait for June.
    We'll all be gone for the summer,
    We're on safari to stay.
    Tell the teacher we're surfin',
    Surfin' U.S.A.

4. At Haggarty's and Swami's
    Pacific Palisades.
    San Onfre and Sunset,
    Redondo Beach L.A.
    All over La Jolla,
    at Waiamea Bay.
    Ev'rybody's gone surfin',
    Surfin' U.S.A.

EASY GUITAR WITH NOTES & TAB

This series features simplified arrangements with notes, tab, chord charts, and strum and pick patterns.

MIXED FOLIOS

00702287 Acoustic	$19.99
00702002 Acoustic Rock Hits for Easy Guitar	$15.99
00702166 All-Time Best Guitar Collection	$19.99
00702232 Best Acoustic Songs for Easy Guitar	$16.99
00119835 Best Children's Songs	$16.99
00703055 The Big Book of Nursery Rhymes & Children's Songs	$16.99
00698978 Big Christmas Collection	$19.99
00702394 Bluegrass Songs for Easy Guitar	$15.99
00289632 Bohemian Rhapsody	$19.99
00703387 Celtic Classics	$14.99
00224808 Chart Hits of 2016-2017	$14.99
00267383 Chart Hits of 2017-2018	$14.99
00334293 Chart Hits of 2019-2020	$16.99
00702149 Children's Christian Songbook	$9.99
00702028 Christmas Classics	$8.99
00101779 Christmas Guitar	$14.99
00702141 Classic Rock	$8.95
00159642 Classical Melodies	$12.99
00253933 Disney/Pixar's Coco	$16.99
00702203 CMT's 100 Greatest Country Songs	$34.99
00702283 The Contemporary Christian Collection	$16.99
00196954 Contemporary Disney	$19.99
00702239 Country Classics for Easy Guitar	$24.99

00702257 Easy Acoustic Guitar Songs	$16.99
00702041 Favorite Hymns for Easy Guitar	$12.99
00222701 Folk Pop Songs	$17.99
00126894 Frozen	$14.99
00333922 Frozen 2	$14.99
00702286 Glee	$16.99
00702160 The Great American Country Songbook	$19.99
00702148 Great American Gospel for Guitar	$14.99
00702050 Great Classical Themes for Easy Guitar	$9.99
00275088 The Greatest Showman	$17.99
00148030 Halloween Guitar Songs	$14.99
00702273 Irish Songs	$12.99
00192503 Jazz Classics for Easy Guitar	$16.99
00702275 Jazz Favorites for Easy Guitar	$17.99
00702274 Jazz Standards for Easy Guitar	$19.99
00702162 Jumbo Easy Guitar Songbook	$24.99
00232285 La La Land	$16.99
00702258 Legends of Rock	$14.99
00702189 MTV's 100 Greatest Pop Songs	$34.99
00702272 1950s Rock	$16.99
00702271 1960s Rock	$16.99
00702270 1970s Rock	$19.99
00702269 1980s Rock	$15.99
00702268 1990s Rock	$19.99
00369043 Rock Songs for Kids	$14.99

00109725 Once	$14.99
00702187 Selections from O Brother Where Art Thou?	$19.99
00702178 100 Songs for Kids	$14.99
00702515 Pirates of the Caribbean	$17.99
00702125 Praise and Worship for Guitar	$14.99
00287930 Songs from *A Star Is Born, The Greatest Showman, La La Land,* and More Movie Musicals	$16.99
00702285 Southern Rock Hits	$12.99
00156420 Star Wars Music	$16.99
00121535 30 Easy Celtic Guitar Solos	$16.99
00702156 3-Chord Rock	$12.99
00244654 Top Hits of 2017	$14.99
00283786 Top Hits of 2018	$14.99
00702294 Top Worship Hits	$17.99
00702255 VH1's 100 Greatest Hard Rock Songs	$34.99
00702175 VH1's 100 Greatest Songs of Rock and Roll	$29.99
00702253 Wicked	$12.99

ARTIST COLLECTIONS

00702267 AC/DC for Easy Guitar	$16.99
00702598 Adele for Easy Guitar	$15.99
00156221 Adele – 25	$16.99
00702040 Best of the Allman Brothers	$16.99
00702865 J.S. Bach for Easy Guitar	$15.99
00702169 Best of The Beach Boys	$15.99
00702292 The Beatles — 1	$22.99
00125796 Best of Chuck Berry	$15.99
00702201 The Essential Black Sabbath	$15.99
00702250 blink-182 — Greatest Hits	$17.99
02501615 Zac Brown Band — The Foundation	$17.99
02501621 Zac Brown Band — You Get What You Give	$16.99
00702043 Best of Johnny Cash	$17.99
00702090 Eric Clapton's Best	$16.99
00702086 Eric Clapton — from the Album Unplugged	$17.99
00702202 The Essential Eric Clapton	$17.99
00702053 Best of Patsy Cline	$15.99
00222697 Very Best of Coldplay – 2nd Edition	$16.99
00702229 The Very Best of Creedence Clearwater Revival	$16.99
00702145 Best of Jim Croce	$16.99
00702278 Crosby, Stills & Nash	$12.99
14042809 Bob Dylan	$15.99
00702276 Fleetwood Mac — Easy Guitar Collection	$17.99
00139462 The Very Best of Grateful Dead	$16.99
00702136 Best of Merle Haggard	$16.99
00702227 Jimi Hendrix — Smash Hits	$19.99
00702288 Best of Hillsong United	$12.99
00702236 Best of Antonio Carlos Jobim	$15.99
00702245 Elton John — Greatest Hits 1970–2002	$19.99

00129855 Jack Johnson	$16.99
00702204 Robert Johnson	$14.99
00702234 Selections from Toby Keith — 35 Biggest Hits	$12.95
00702003 Kiss	$16.99
00702216 Lynyrd Skynyrd	$16.99
00702182 The Essential Bob Marley	$16.99
00146081 Maroon 5	$14.99
00121925 Bruno Mars – Unorthodox Jukebox	$12.99
00702248 Paul McCartney — All the Best	$14.99
00125484 The Best of MercyMe	$12.99
00702209 Steve Miller Band — Young Hearts (Greatest Hits)	$12.95
00124167 Jason Mraz	$15.99
00702096 Best of Nirvana	$16.99
00702211 The Offspring — Greatest Hits	$17.99
00138026 One Direction	$17.99
00702030 Best of Roy Orbison	$17.99
00702144 Best of Ozzy Osbourne	$14.99
00702279 Tom Petty	$17.99
00102911 Pink Floyd	$17.99
00702139 Elvis Country Favorites	$19.99
00702293 The Very Best of Prince	$19.99
00699415 Best of Queen for Guitar	$16.99
00109279 Best of R.E.M.	$14.99
00702208 Red Hot Chili Peppers — Greatest Hits	$16.99
00198960 The Rolling Stones	$17.99
00174793 The Very Best of Santana	$16.99
00702196 Best of Bob Seger	$16.99
00146046 Ed Sheeran	$15.99
00702252 Frank Sinatra — Nothing But the Best	$12.99
00702010 Best of Rod Stewart	$17.99
00702049 Best of George Strait	$17.99

00702259 Taylor Swift for Easy Guitar	$15.99
00359800 Taylor Swift – Easy Guitar Anthology	$24.99
00702260 Taylor Swift — Fearless	$14.99
00139727 Taylor Swift — 1989	$17.99
00115960 Taylor Swift — Red	$16.99
00253667 Taylor Swift — Reputation	$17.99
00702290 Taylor Swift — Speak Now	$16.99
00232849 Chris Tomlin Collection – 2nd Edition	$14.99
00702226 Chris Tomlin — See the Morning	$12.95
00148643 Train	$14.99
00702427 U2 — 18 Singles	$19.99
00702108 Best of Stevie Ray Vaughan	$17.99
00279005 The Who	$14.99
00702123 Best of Hank Williams	$15.99
00194548 Best of John Williams	$14.99
00702228 Neil Young — Greatest Hits	$17.99
00119133 Neil Young — Harvest	$14.99

Prices, contents and availability
subject to change without notice.

Visit Hal Leonard online at **halleonard.com**

1221
306